Exploring the World of Geology

TRY THIS !

by George Burns

illustrated by Nancy Woodman

A *Try This* Book

Franklin Watts

A Division of Grolier Publishing

New York ✺ London ✺ Hong Kong ✺ Sydney

Danbury, Connecticut

For Lisa
—George Burns

To David, an igneous
metamorphic enigma
—Nancy Woodman

Cover illustration by Nancy Woodman

Photographs copyright ©: Photo Researchers: pp. 4 (Simon Fraser/SPL),
7 (John Buitenkant), 12 (Soames Summerhays), 24 (Francois Gohier),
36 (David Parker/SPL), 44 (Krafft-Explorer); U.S. Geological Survey, Photographic
Library, Denver, CO: pp. 16 (W. B. Hamilton), 33; Ward's Natural Science
Establishment, Inc.: pp. 17, 18, 19, 23, 28; Comstock/Russ Kinne: p. 40.

Library of Congress Cataloging-in-Publication Data

Burns, George, 1952–
Exploring the world of geology / by George Burns;
illustrated by Nancy Woodman.
p. cm. — (Try this series)
Includes bibliographical references and index.
Summary: Suggests simple activities for exploring geology,
the study of the land covering our planet.
ISBN 0-531-20121-X
1. Geology—Experiments—Juvenile literature. [1. Geology—Experiments.
2. Experiments.] I. Woodman, Nancy, ill. II. Title. III. Series.
QE29.B93 1995
551'.078—dc20
95-9538
CIP AC

CONTENTS

*Because of its geology, Iceland has a lot of volcanoes
and many earthquakes. These cliffs came from the movement
of two large plates of rock underneath Iceland.*

THE WORLD OF GEOLOGY

If you're like most people, you've dug a hole in the ground at some point during your life. But have you ever wondered what you would find if you kept on digging? Or just how far down you could go?

And how about rocks? Have you ever noticed that some rocks can be perfectly smooth and very beautiful while others are very jagged and rough? How do rocks come to be the way they are?

Have you ever wondered why the earth shakes under our feet during earthquakes, or what causes the fiery explosions inside volcanoes? If you have ever asked yourself questions like these, then you have already taken your first steps toward becoming a *geologist*. (To learn how to pronounce any word in italics look in the glossary at the back of this book.)

Geology is the study of all the land covering the earth. Geologists study the very ground we walk upon and everything underneath it. They try to understand what causes the land to move suddenly during earthquakes and volcanic eruptions. They also study how it has moved and changed very slowly over many centuries.

Geologists know that rocks hold the secrets of the history of the earth. Rocks underground can also give clues to the people and other living things from many, many years ago.

To begin being a geologist, all you really need to do is to start exploring and carefully observing the land around you. This book will give you simple and interesting ways to begin your explorations.

One thing professional geologists do is keep careful records of their work. You may want to get a notebook or pad to keep track of all the things you do while exploring. Be a geologist and try these activities!

DIGGING DIRT

A good way to start being a geologist is to sift through some earth, or soil. At first, soil may not seem very interesting. Most people avoid it because they don't want to get dirty. In fact, soil is often called dirt. But dirt

Red soil in California

isn t all bad. If it didn't exist, we wouldn't have the food that grows in soil. If you take some time to look at dirt, you may discover many wonderful things about it.

Some soils are a deep, dark brown. A handful of this kind of soil feels rich and moist and crumbles softly in your hand. Other soils are a beautiful red, baking in the sun. Although this kind of soil may be hard and dry, it is silky and warm to the touch. One of the most appealing things about dirt is all the surprises you can find in it.

Try This:

You can do this activity in your own backyard, in a nearby field, or anywhere you can dig a good hole in the ground. Wherever you decide to do it, make sure it's all right to be digging there. Ask permission from your parents or whoever happens to own the land.

Get a trowel or a stick and start digging. What do you find in your hole? You may find some worms or old cans. Or you may find something very unusual, like an animal bone. But you will also probably find a lot of dirt and rocks. Save them for the next few activities. For now, think about this question: What is dirt?

Do this activity outside. Fill a glass jar half full of soil. Make sure there are no large rocks in the jar. Small ones are okay. Fill the rest of the jar with water. Screw the lid on tightly and carefully shake the jar up and down and all around. Shake it for at least two minutes or until all the soil has mixed with the water.

Now hold the jar with both hands and let it hang down in front of you. Carefully and slowly swing the jar back and forth as though your arms were a playground swing. Do this for about two minutes. Then take the jar inside and let it sit for a couple of hours.

After everything in the jar has settled and the water is clear again, take a good look at the soil through the side of the jar. Does it look different in any way? Do you notice layers of different kinds of materials? Draw a picture of what you see on loose paper or in your notebook. Label it with the date and the location of your hole.

Soil is made up of many different materials. You probably found large and small rocks in the soil when you were digging. But soil also contains rocky pieces that are much smaller than any pebbles you found. These pieces come from rocky material that has been broken down over very long periods of time. This rocky material is made of *minerals*.

Soil also contains material from plants and animals. For example, it might contain roots, leaves, pieces of wood, bone, decayed flesh, and waste matter. Material from living things is called *organic material*.

The organic material mixes with the rocky material in the soil and creates a rich environment for living things. That is why you may have found roots, bugs, or worms living in your soil. Plants and bugs use the organic material as food to help them grow. People look for soil containing lots of organic material when they plant gardens or crops.

Did the soil in your jar look the same after the experiment? When water is added to soil, the heavier, rocky material falls toward the bottom of the jar. The lighter, finer pieces float or settle on the top of the soil. Medium-sized grains of rock settle in the middle.

If your soil contains a good mixture of materials, you should see a series of layers in your jar. Each layer is made up of one of the materials found in soil. The particles in each layer are about the same size and weight.

Do this activity with soil from different locations. Draw the layers you get from each location in your notebook. Remember to write down the location and the date next to each drawing. Then compare the layers in each drawing.

Keep on Digging

The hole you made is probably only as deep as your arm is long. It may be a little less or a little more than that. But what would happen if you kept digging? Suppose you had a great big shovel and lots of muscle. What would you find if you just kept digging and digging and digging?

Depending upon where you live, you might actually dig through the soil pretty quickly. But the soil is just one of the layers that make up the earth. After many yards (or meters) of soil, you would eventually hit the layer of the earth called the *crust*. The crust is a hard layer of rock anywhere from 10 to 25 miles (16 to 40 kilometers) thick.

If you could dig through the crust, you would come to a much thicker layer of rock called the *mantle*. The mantle is about 1,800 miles (2,900 km) thick. It is so hot that in many places the rock has melted into liquid. Sometimes the molten rock bursts up through the surface in a volcano.

And if you could somehow dig through all that hot rock, you would come to a thick layer called the *outer core*. Here we have a layer of metal so hot that it is melted, or molten. The thickness of this layer is about 1,380 miles (2,220 km).

Molten rock from the earth's mantle flows from a volcano in Hawaii.

Finally, after a lot of digging and heat, you would arrive at the *inner core*. This is the very center of the earth. The inner core is made of solid metal but is extremely hot. It has temperatures as high as 7,000° F (almost 4,000° C).

Nobody has ever been able to dig that deep. So you probably wouldn't get very far with your shovel. But you can easily create a model of the inside of the earth instead.

Try This:

Make the layers of the earth from modeling clay or play dough. If possible, use a different color for each layer. Start by rolling a ball of clay about an inch (or 2 1/2 centimeters) thick. This will be the inner core.

Roll the other layers out flat on a table using a rolling pin or a pillar from a set of building blocks. First

roll a round slab of clay that is about 4 inches (10 cm) across and 3/4 of an inch (2 cm) thick. Shape it into a bowl and put the inner core in the middle of it. This bowl will be the outer core.

Wrap the outer core around the inner core as closely as possible. But don't squeeze it too much. The outer core has to go only about halfway around the ball.

Roll out a round slab of clay of another color. Make it about 6 inches (15 cm) across and about 1 inch (2 1/2 cm) thick. Shape it into a bowl and fit the two cores inside it. This will be the mantle. It should look like a ball inside a bowl, inside a larger bowl.

Now roll out a very skinny, round layer of clay about the same size as the mantle. It doesn't have to be a new color, but it should be a different color from the mantle. Make the clay no thicker than a piece of cardboard. Wrap it around the bowl of the mantle. This will be the crust.

For the last layer, roll out a round slab of clay about as thin as a piece of paper. This will be the layer of soil that covers the earth. Wrap it around the crust.

To get a good view of all your layers, slice through the clay with a butter knife. Carefully cut out a section of your model as though you were cutting out a wedge in an apple. Don't press too hard on the knife as you slice. If you do, you could squeeze the shape out of your model.

Your wedge of clay should show you a good *cross section* of your model of the earth. It lets you see how the layers look from the surface to the center of your model. Draw a picture to go along with your model. Label the different layers of the earth.

THE SECRETS IN ROCKS

You have learned that a great deal of the earth is made of rock. But what is rock? Where do rocks come from?

Slate from the Great Smoky Mountains of Tennessee.

There are three ways that rocks can form. *Igneous rocks* form after minerals become so hot that they melt together. This happens deep in the crust and in the mantle, as you read in Chapter 2. As the molten rock is gradually pushed up toward the surface of the earth, the rock cools and hardens. *Granite* is one kind of igneous rock.

Granite

Obsidian

Gabbro

Igneous rocks

Other rocks are formed by the tremendous pressure and heat deep within the crust of the earth. The minerals do not actually melt. But they are pressed together so hard that they change into a new substance. These are called *metamorphic rocks*. *Slate* is a good example of a metamorphic rock.

Gneiss

Schist

Pink quartzite

Metamorphic rocks

And then there are rocks that are created by water and wind at the surface of the earth. Water and wind drag minerals and organic material over the land. When the materials finally settle into one spot, they become hard over time. They build in layers, one on top of the other. These are called *sedimentary rocks. Sandstone* is one kind of sedimentary rock.

The best way to begin learning about the different kinds of rocks is to start a rock collection. No matter where you live, you will always be able to find rocks around you. It may not be easy to find unusual rocks. But you will usually be able to find very beautiful ones. See whether you can guess how they were formed.

Sandstone

Conglomerate

Limestone

Sedimentary rocks

Try This:

You can start your collection with the rocks from the hole you dug. Look for more rocks in your yard or nearby park. You might be able to find some in your schoolyard or on the way to school. If you can go to some woods or a stream, you should be able to find plenty of rocks.

Be sure to ask permission if you are collecting on someone else's property. And don't collect rocks from rock gardens. Vacations are a good time to add to your rock collection. You can usually find new kinds of rocks if you travel to a different place.

Wash off your rocks and let them dry. Then try putting similar rocks together. You might want to group them according to color, shape, or size. Or you could organize them according to the material in the rock. Look at the material very closely. Is the rock made of material that is easy to break off or scrape off? Does the rock look glassy? Is it layered? Is it made of smaller pieces of rock stuck together?

When you have decided how you want to organize your rocks, get a box for each group. You could use shoe boxes, cigar boxes, or any other small boxes. Label each box with the type of rock. Some labels you might use are:

Smooth, glassy rocks
Rocks I can break with my hands
Rocks with visible particles
Rocks with layers

To keep track of your rocks, you may want to put a small piece of masking tape on each one. Give each rock a number and write it on the tape. Keep a list of all your rocks in your notebook. Next to each rock number, write a description of the rock and where you found it. If you have a field guide to rocks, try to identify your rocks.

It is not always easy to tell whether you have an igneous, metamorphic, or sedimentary rock just by look-ing at it. If there are tiny specks of black or color in a smooth rock, you probably have an igneous rock. If the rock is made up of particles, you probably have a sedi-

mentary rock. Metamorphic rocks have many of the characteristics of both igneous and sedimentary rocks.

A good way to find out which kinds of rocks you have is to learn about the geology of the land where you live. Some areas of the country have only one or two kinds of rock because of the way the land formed there. Ask your teacher what kind of geology your state has.

A field guide to rocks can also help you find out what kind of rock you have. Look through the pictures for your rock. This guide should tell you to which of the three classes it belongs.

If you really enjoy collecting rocks, you might want to save up your money for a geologist's hammer and a pair of goggles. With the hammer, you can break open rocks or chip away at a large rock. Always wear goggles over your eyes when you do this and do it away from other people. Rock particles can fly into the air and hit you or someone nearby. Also, you should never try to break up rocks with a regular hammer. You could ruin the hammer, and it wouldn't work anyway.

Traces of Life in Rocks

All the things that geologists discover in the earth are clues to our planet's history. The clues can help us understand what the earth is like right now and what it will be like in the future. Some things geologists find may be clues to the history of living things, including plants, animals, and people. A fossil is a good example of this kind of discovery.

What is a fossil? Fossils are traces of living things in rocks. The outline of a fish skeleton pressed into stone is a fossil. How does that happen? When a fish dies, its body sinks to the ocean, river, or lake floor. Dirt and dust falling through the water begin to cover it like a blanket. If the body is covered quickly enough, it cannot rot or get swept away.

The falling material, called *sediment*, is the same stuff that hardens into rock over many, many years. As it hardens, the fish's bones begin dissolving and minerals in the rock take their place. These minerals become a perfect copy of the fish skeleton printed permanently into the rock!

A fossil of a fish in limestone

Many years later the water in the lake or ocean might dry up. Or an erupting volcano might bring part of the sea floor above water. Then a geologist may dig down and uncover the fossil. Or wind and rain could expose it.

Fossils can also be made by a seashell, a plant, or even an animal's footprint. Scientists who study fossils are called *paleontologists*. Fossils help them figure out what kinds of plants and animals lived on the earth long ago. Everything we know about dinosaurs comes from fossils. They have even taught us about the first tiny animals to live on the earth millions of years ago.

Fossils are amazing things. If you are having trouble understanding how they are formed, making a model of a fossil might help.

*This mountain is made of layers of rock
that formed when sediment hardened.*

Try This:

Your fossils won't take nearly as long to make as real fossils. First find something that you want to turn into a fossil. A seashell or a chicken or fish bone would work very well.

The simplest model of a fossil can be made with clay. You should use regular clay, not modeling clay. Roll out a slab of clay about 1/2 inch (1 1/4 cm) thick. Make sure it is larger than your seashell or bone. Then press

the object care-
fully into the slab
of clay. If it
doesn't sink into
the clay easily,
wet the slab with
a little bit of
water.

Now remove
the object and
let the clay dry
out. This may take a day. When it is dry, your model is
ready to be painted. Be sure to handle it carefully. Dried
clay is very brittle and breaks easily. If you can, fire it in
a kiln so that it becomes harder and stronger.

Use poster paint and a thin paintbrush to color in
the impression left by the shell or bone. Brown or
another dark color works well. Think of the paint as
minerals that take the place of the shell or bone. You

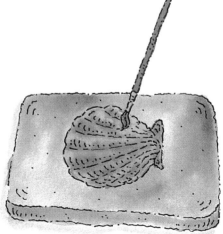

can probably paint the impression in less than ten minutes. But in real fossils it takes many, many years for minerals to replace bone.

Try This:

Another way to make a model of a fossil is with plaster of Paris. You can make the model in a paper or styrofoam tray from a package of grocery meat. Be sure to wash the meat tray thoroughly before you use it.

In a bowl, mix enough plaster of Paris to fill the meat tray. The mixture should not be too wet. Pour the mixture into the meat tray so that the surface of the plaster is nice and smooth. Before making your impression, the plaster should feel about as hard as wet clay. If it is too soft or mushy, let it dry out for awhile.

Rub petroleum jelly on a bone or a shell. This will keep it from getting stuck in the plaster. Push the bone or shell into the plaster without letting the plaster cover any part of it.

Let the plaster dry. It may take a few hours or more.

Then carefully pull out the bone or shell. This fossil will be harder than a clay fossil dried in the air.

Now make another mixture of plaster of Paris. This time mix in a few drops of red, yellow, and blue food coloring. The plaster should now be dark in color.

Carefully pour this mixture into the shape left by your shell or bone in the meat tray. Scrape off any excess plaster by sliding a butter knife over the top of the model. Then let the plaster sit. When it is completely dry, you will have a model of your shell or bone that looks just like a fossil in stone.

You may want to draw the fossils you made on paper or in your note-book. You can also create a story about when the animal lived and how it became a fossil.

WHEN THE EARTH MOVES

How do tall mountains become humble hills? How do little streams become deep rivers? Water and air are continually changing the surface of the earth. They move over the land and wear it away. This is called *erosion*.

Wind blowing sand against this rock eroded it, making the holes you see.

Erosion sometimes happens very quickly—in floods and hurricanes, for example. But more often, it takes hundreds or thousands or even millions of years to change the face of the earth.

Luckily, there is a way to see how erosion works in much less time.

Try This:

Find a patch of bare dirt outside on the ground. With a stick, scratch a big rectangle in the dirt. If there is no dirt patch you can use, fill a wooden or plastic box with dirt instead.

You are going to "erode" the dirt by blowing on it through a cardboard tube from a roll of paper towels or toilet paper. You can also force air over the dirt with a bicycle pump if you have one. It works better than blowing through a tube.

But before you do anything to your area of dirt, take a good look at it. Try to remember what it looks like. Are there rocks or twigs on it? Are there roots sticking out of the ground? You may want to draw pictures of it in your notebook now and at each step of this activity.

When you are ready, start blowing through the tube on the dirt (or use the pump). Try blowing hard and then blowing softly. Try putting the tube close to the dirt and then far away. Can you create enough wind to move the dirt around?

What happens when you blow for a long time on one spot? Can you make a little valley in the dirt? If you're having trouble moving the dirt, get some friends to help you blow on it.

Compare your patch of dirt now with the way it looked before. Has your wind changed it much? If it has, that's erosion. Draw a picture of the patch in your notebook.

Do this activity on the same patch of dirt from the previous activity. This time you can save your breath and let water do the work. Hold a garden hose over the dirt and turn on the water. Keep a steady stream of water flowing over your patch of dirt. If you don't have a hose, you can use a pitcher of water or a plant spray bottle instead. Refill the pitcher and pour the water on the same spot over and over again.

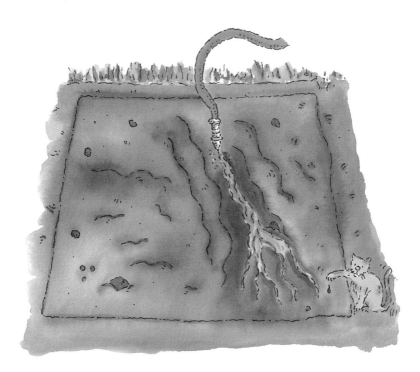

What's happening to the dirt? What happens when you spray harder? Can you make a path in the dirt with the water?

Let the dirt dry out and then take another look at it. Compare your patch of dirt now with the way it looked before. Have your wind and water eroded it?

You may not have flattened any mountains or worn away any boulders. That takes nature a long time. But if you could keep blowing and spraying for a few thousand years, you might very well end up with a river bed in your backyard!

Erupting Volcanoes

Sometimes the earth's surface changes very suddenly because of activity deep within the earth. One way that happens is in a volcano.

You read in Chapter 2 that the molten rock in the mantle sometimes rushes up to the surface of the earth. This liquid rock, also called magma, is under great pressure and is incredibly hot. Every once in a while, the magma breaks through a weak spot in the earth's crust. It bursts out into the air through a hole at the top of a mound or a mountain.

This is the *eruption* of a volcano. When the magma spews forth from the volcano, it is called *lava*.

You can watch heat and pressure cause similar, very tiny eruptions in your kitchen.

Try This:

First you must get an adult's permission to cook some oatmeal on the stove. Have an adult help you do this activity.

Mount St. Helens, a volcano in Washington, erupted in 1980.

Pour 1-1/2 cups of water into a medium-size pot with a handle. Add 2/3 cup of oatmeal and set it on a burner of the stove over medium heat. Bring the water to a boil.

While the oatmeal is cooking, pour a very thin layer of water—about 1 to 2 tablespoons—into another pot. The water should just cover the bottom of the pot. Add a few drops of red food coloring—and a few drops of yellow, if you have it—and then mix. This will be your magma.

When the oatmeal begins to boil, lower the heat. Stir it occasionally as it cooks and watch it closely. When it begins to thicken, turn on the heat under the second pot. It should heat up quickly. You should soon start to notice some volcanic action in the oatmeal. As

Oatmeal + Water   Food Coloring + Water

the water at the bottom of the oatmeal pot gets hot, it forces its way up through the oatmeal in little bursts.

As soon as the oatmeal starts looking like lots of little volcanoes, turn off the burner underneath it. Carefully pour the oatmeal from the first pot into the pot with the red water. Do not stir the oatmeal into the water. Watch carefully as the oatmeal volcanoes continue to burst through.

Now, however, you should start to see little bursts of red liquid coming out of the volcanoes. This red liquid represents lava. For this activity to work properly, it is important that you pour the oatmeal before it gets too thick.

Remember to turn off the heat when the liquid has boiled away. If you don't, the oatmeal could burn. The oatmeal is safe to eat, if you want it. Don't forget to clean the pots when you are finished.

If the red water at the bottom of the pot was magma, then what was the oatmeal?

The oatmeal is like the earth's crust. A long time ago, the earth probably looked a lot like your pot of volcanoes. When the earth was very young, it had many

more active, or erupting, volcanoes. Today most volcanoes on the earth are not active.

Shaking and Quaking

There is still another way that the earth can move violently. It has to do with enormous slabs of rock, called *plates,* in the earth's crust. These plates are so large that some are bigger than the entire United States. They fit together like pieces of a gigantic puzzle that covers the earth. The land we live on rests on these plates.

The plates move very, very slowly. In a year, they may travel only a few inches. Even so, sometimes the plates push up against each other with great force. The plates may jerk suddenly, crushing rocks below or forcing them to slide past each other. When this happens,

This rift in the ground in California was caused by the San Andreas fault, where two large plates of rock meet underground.

the people living on the land above feel the rumblings of an *earthquake.*

You can build a model of the plates, the land, and a building resting on it. The model will give you a good idea of what an earthquake is and how it works.

You can make an earthquake model with a set of building blocks.

First, lay two long blocks next to each other. Push them together so that they touch along their lengths. Think of

them as the edges of two plates that meet underground. Geologists call this meeting line a *fault.*

Place two or three long blocks on top of the first two in the other direction. You should now have something that looks like a big plus sign. Think of the blocks on top as land above the plates. Place a small building on top of the land.

Now hold onto the two blocks on bottom. Slowly pull them so that they slide past each other. What happens to your building and the land below? This is the sort of earthquake that occurs when two plates slide sideways against each other. Plates can also slide up and down against each other.

More sudden and powerful earthquakes can occur when rocks are wedged in between plates.

Try This:

Put a square block in between the first two blocks of the previous activity. Turn the block at an angle so that two of its corners touch the long blocks. Think of the square block as a huge rock wedged between two plates.

Push two more long blocks against the bottom blocks. One end of each new block should rest against the middle of one of the first blocks. These new blocks will be used to squeeze the plates against the rock. Place land and a building on top of the plates as in the previous activity.

Push the two new blocks toward each other so that the plates squeeze the rock. It may be hard to move them together at first. But as the square block turns, the plates will move and an earthquake should occur beneath your building.

Try making buildings of different sizes. How are they affected by your earthquakes? See whether you can design a building that stands up pretty well during an earthquake.

THE WONDROUS EARTH

The planet we live on is extraordinary for many reasons. One of the most incredible things about the earth is its *magnetism*.

Magnetism is a force that attracts iron. You may have seen magnets decorating refrigerators. The magnetism in these magnets pulls them toward the iron in the refrigerator door.

The earth itself is an enormous magnet. It has a north and south pole at opposite ends just like all magnets do. If you have a strong magnet, you can use it to understand the earth's magnetism.

A mineral called magnetite acts like a magnet.

Look around your house and try to guess which objects a magnet will attract. Make a list of the objects in your notebook. Then get a magnet and try it on each one. Check off the objects that are attracted by the magnet. Do they have anything in common?

Most of the earth's magnetism comes from its iron core. So the earth's magnet is located mainly in its center. As in all magnets, the magnetism extends outward into the surrounding space. Scientists call this region of magnetic force a *magnetic field*.

That's how a magnet attracts nearby objects that are not even touching it. It attracts anything that happens to be within the magnetic field. If an object has any iron in it, it moves toward the magnet. Objects far away from the magnet are not attracted because they are outside the *magnetic field*.

You can see how this works for yourself in the next activity.

Hold a magnet out in front of you. Place a single paper clip on it and let it hang there. Now try hanging another paper clip from the end of the first one. Just let the clip touch and see if it sticks. Then try attaching a third paper clip to the second one.

See how long a line of paper clips you can make. The stronger the magnet, the longer the line will be. That's because the magnetism from a stronger magnet spreads further into the surrounding space.

While the paper clips are in the magnetic field, they act just like magnets themselves. But there is a way to make the clips remain magnets even when they are removed from the magnetic field.

Try This:

Get a sewing needle or pin and rub it against your magnet. Start at the head of the pin and move toward the point. Rub the pin in this direction many times. To avoid rubbing in the reverse direction, lift the pin after each stroke. Then check to see if the pin attracts other pins. If it does, you have created a very skinny magnet. You have magnetized the pin. The more you rub the pin, the stronger your magnet will be. See if the same thing happens with a nail.

In a similar way, the earth's magnetic field magnetizes a mineral found in some rocks. It is called *magnetite*, and it is found throughout the earth's crust. Magnetite becomes magnetized because it has iron in it.

The earth's magnetism also reaches us on the surface of the earth. There are two reasons we don't notice it. We have only a tiny bit of iron inside us. And the magnetism is weak compared to your magnet because we are so far from the earth's core.

If you have a compass, you can see the power of the earth's magnetism around you. Hold it horizontally in front of you. The compass needle lines up with the earth's magnetic field by pointing toward the North Pole. That's because the needle is magnetized.

With a strong magnet, it is easy to make your own compass.

Try This:

Get a small circle of cork or styrofoam. Put it in a bowl of water and watch it float. Notice which side faces up. Take the floating disk out of the water and carefully tape the magnetized sewing pin across the top side. Then place it back in the water.

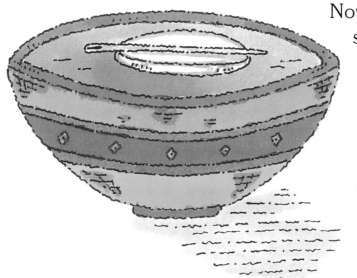

Now the disk should turn in the water until the needle tip points to the north.

After finishing the activities in this book, try going back to the hole that you dug. You can now look at it with the eyes of a more experienced geologist. Your knowledge may help you see many new things.

Lava from a volcano in Zaire hardens into rock.

What else would you like to know about what's inside and on top of the earth? Keep your notebook to record any interesting observations you make in the future and any questions that come up.

Whenever you go someplace new, take time to look at the land and rocks you see there. Take some samples, and add them to your rock collection. Keep your eyes open and keep on digging. Who knows—you could uncover some secrets in the earth.

GLOSSARY

crust (krust)—the hard layer of the earth that is just below the land—the soil.

cross section (cross-SEK-shun)—a view of the inside of an object. In other words, the view that would appear if you cut through the middle of the object.

earthquake (EARTH-kwake)—sudden vibrations of the ground caused by the movement of the plates in the earth's crust.

erosion (ih-ROW-jhun)—the wearing away of the earth's surface by wind and water.

eruption (ih-RUP-shun)—the bursting of magma through the earth's crust and out the top of a volcano.

fault (fault)—a break in the crust of the earth that can sometimes cause earthquakes. Beneath the fault, plates of rock rub against each other.

fossil (FOSS-uhl)—an impression of a dead plant or animal inside rock in the earth's crust. Geologists study fossils to learn about plants and animals from long ago.

geologist (jee-OL-uh-jist)—a person who studies land, rocks, volcanoes, earthquakes, and the history of the earth.

granite (GRAN-it)—a very hard igneous rock used at the base of buildings to make them strong.

igneous (IG-nee-us) **rock**—rock formed from minerals that have melted completely.

inner core—the very center of the earth, where temperatures are extremely high. It is made of liquid metal at 7,000°F.

lava (LAH-vuh)—magma that has burst through the top of a volcano.

magma (MAG-muh)—molten rock within the earth.

magnetic (mag-NET-ik) **field**—a space in which magnetic force is present.

magnetism (MAG-nuh-ti-zum)—the attraction for iron produced by a magnet.

mantle (MAN-tull)—the hot layer of the earth below the crust, where rock is melted in places.

metamorphic (met-uh-MORE-fik) **rock**—rock formed as a result of pressure and heat, rather than melting.

minerals (MIN-er-uhls)—materials found underground and in rocks. They do not come from living things—plants or animals. They may be elements, such as copper and gold, or they could be combinations of elements. Quartz, graphite, talc, and diamond are minerals.

molten (MOLE-ton)—completely melted. It usually describes a hard solid such as rock or metal that has become so hot, it has turned to liquid.

organic (or-GAN-ik) material—material from living things—plants or animals.

outer core—the layer of the earth between the inner core and mantle. It is made of liquid metal.

paleontologist (pay-lee-on-TAL-uh-jist)—a scientist who studies fossils to learn about the history of life on earth.

plates—enormous slabs of rock in the earth's crust that the continents rest on.

sandstone (SAND-stone)—a sedimentary rock that looks like it's made up of tiny particles of sand.

sediment (SED-uh-ment)—particles of dirt and dust that sink to the bottom of rivers, lakes, and oceans. The wind also scatters it over the land.

sedimentary (said-uh-MENT-uh-ree) **rock**—rock formed by the buildup and hardening of dirt and dust particles. The particles build in layers, which are often seen along the sides of roads that have been cut through rocks.

slate (slate)—a dark gray metamorphic rock that can be easily split apart in sheets. It is often used in roofs.

INDEX

Page numbers in *italics* indicate illustrations.